# ABC Cookery

## SUNNY
## COURINGTON
## STEPHENS

**ARGUS COMMUNICATIONS**
A Division of **DLM,** Inc.
Niles, Illinois 60648 U.S.A.

**FIRST EDITION**

© Copyright 1979 Argus Communications

Printed in the United States of America.

**ARGUS COMMUNICATIONS**
A Division of **DLM,** Inc.
Niles, Illinois 60648 U.S.A.

International Standard Book Number: 0-89505-024-2
Library of Congress Number: 79-63173

0 9 8 7 6 5 4 3

*A way to your child's mind
through his stomach*

# Contents

Applesauce . . . . . . . . . 12

Butter . . . . . . . . . . . . 16

Cocoa . . . . . . . . . . . 20

Doughnuts . . . . . . . . . 24

English Toffee . . . . . . . . 28

Fudge . . . . . . . . . . . 32

Gingerbread Man . . . . . . 36

Hotcakes . . . . . . . . . . 40

Ice Cream . . . . . . . . . 44

Jell-O . . . . . . . . . . . 48

Kisses . . . . . . . . . . . 52

Lemonade . . . . . . . . . 56

Marshmallow Candy . . . . . 60

No-Bake Nuggets . . . . . . 64

Oatmeal Drink . . . . . . . . . 68

Popcorn . . . . . . . . . . . . 72

Quick Muffins . . . . . . . . 76

Raisin Rocks . . . . . . . . 80

Sandwich . . . . . . . . . . 84

Toast . . . . . . . . . . . . 88

Upside Down Cake . . . . . . 92

Vegetable Soup . . . . . . . . 96

Watermelon . . . . . . . . . 100

X-tra Recipes . . . . . . . 104
   Chocolate Pudding . . . . . 105
   Shortcake . . . . . . . . . 107
   Thumbprint Cookies . . . . 110
   Wheatgerm Bread . . . . . 113

Yeast Biscuits . . . . . . . . 116

Zoo Cookies . . . . . . . . . 120

# Introduction

"The best educational toy is a parent," it's been said. And parents know that there's more than an ounce of truth to that statement!

Parents, of course, have much to do with how the "seedling" that becomes a "tree" is nourished, with respect to learning as well as food. They influence a child's attitudes, his or her emotional, physical, and social development, and in many instances the extent to which a child acquires skills that will serve in everyday living and in school.

A child learns in many settings, outside and inside the home. But have you ever thought of the kitchen—that room in which love is expressed through meal preparation—as an ideal learning center? Have you ever considered how experiences in the kitchen can further a child's development in many ways, and that by sharing experiences there, you can help prepare your child for school and for life?

As a place to learn, the kitchen is uniquely qualified. It is a warm, friendly, relaxed spot, full of nice smells and good things to eat. It's comfortable. Tools for learning are all around—spoons, bowls, measuring and mixing devices, and so on. A variety of ingredients are available. And the child's participation in following recipes to make sauces, muffins, candies, and other simple foods becomes the vehicle for learning.

Messy? It can be, at least a little. Let's admit that right off. There occasionally might be some spilled milk, a counter grainy with salt or sugar, an egg fallen humpty-dumpty on the floor. When involving a child in the kitchen, one suspends a tender regard for tidiness and efficiency. Even under the best of circumstances, cooking involves some mess. Learning to be careful and to take responsibility for cleaning up is also part of the growing process. Children like nothing better than participation; from curiosity and accomplishment comes learning. And learning is what children are about—that activity consumes most of their waking hours.

How loosely or closely you guide your child, as the two of you combine the ingredients of a recipe into something good to eat, is up to you. It also depends on your child's stage of development. You might agree with the philosophy: "You can't teach children to take care of themselves unless you will *let them try* to take care of themselves. They will make mistakes; and out of these mistakes will come their wisdom." Or, you might believe that firm control and direction works best, preferring more structured situations in the case of you and your child. Either way, there's still a lot to be learned in the kitchen.

What kinds of learning are we talking about?

Learning, as we know, clusters in certain categories. They are not mutually exclusive classifications, though; they may frequently overlap. But for purposes of discussion, these learnings, which one might call skills, will be isolated.

One category is motor skills. There are two kinds. One is gross, or large motor skills, referring to movement of large bones and muscles. The other is fine, or small motor skills, engaging smaller muscles and bones, such as those in the hand.

The ability to walk, run, jump, ride a tricycle or a bicycle, all indicate progress in the development of large motor skills.

Small motor skills are used in performing tasks such as lacing a shoe or threading a needle. And activities engaging skills such as these require a working relationship between hands and eyes, which child development specialists call "hand-eye coordination."

Developing motor skills, particularly the fine ones, gives a child greater control over his environment. At the same time, such achievements represent milestones along the path toward a greater degree of independence. Mastery is liberating. The ability to feed and dress oneself, tie one's shoelaces, and so on means less dependence on others for normal, everyday functions. And as accomplishment increases, so does self-esteem.

Many motor skills are related to other kinds of skills. A child who can grasp and pick up an object for closer examination will gain more knowledge about it than one who cannot. Speech is possible only after a child can control and coordinate mouth and tongue muscles. A child is not ready to learn to print until he or she can control a pencil or a crayon well enough to make appropriate marks on paper. Reading is difficult unless the eyes are trained to move from left to right.

Motor skills is one area of learning. Language is a second.

Children quickly realize that the world into which they are born attaches great importance to symbols. And they soon learn that the greatest bundle of symbols with which they will deal is language— a means of making known needs and wants, conveying feelings and desires, thinking, gaining knowledge, and connecting past, present, and future.

Language development seems a natural thing. This does not mean, however, that a parent should not help it along, any more than one

should refrain from helping a toddler learn to walk—another natural development. The more words and sentences a child hears and practices, the greater his or her vocabulary. This leads, in turn, to a greater capacity for verbal communication and to improved thinking skills. By following suggestions contained in this book, you'll have plenty of opportunities to help your child further develop language skills.

Our third category of learning is cognitive skills.

A dictionary will define cognition as a means of acquiring knowledge, or the ability to solve written or verbal problems. Many people, consequently, think of cognitive skills in terms of reading, writing, and arithmetic. True, there is a relationship between cognition and knowledge and understanding. But "cognitive skills" also refer to something else, equally important.

More precisely, cognitive skills relate to an ability to make sense of, or to sort out, jumbled masses of information, knowledge, or sensation—the process of classifying items of experiences. Put another way, cognitive skill involves molding bits and pieces into patterns, using parts to make wholes and establish relationships.

What are some of the specifics your child might learn and practice while engaging in activities in the kitchen?

With regard to motor skills, there will be opportunities for pushing and pulling a rolling pin, for stirring with a large wooden spoon, sifting flour, and mixing ingredients by shaking. Other activities include pouring, patting, unwrapping, kneading, opening packages, and unscrewing and replacing jar lids.

Every activity involves conversation and following directions. In preparing these recipes, the child will encounter the letters of the alphabet. He or she will absorb new words while learning to identify kitchen utensils, equipment, and the ingredients of recipes. There will be opportunities to "show and tell" as you and your child discuss what you have done while you both enjoy good things to eat. These experiences all help develop language skills.

Being able to relate what has occurred involves the cognitive skills of remembering and placing events in sequence. At the same time, there will be opportunities to deal with such concepts as number, quantity, hot-cold, liquid-solid, top-bottom, and geometrical shapes.

Identifying colors, tastes and smells are also cognitive experiences, as is learning to recognize letters of the alphabet.

Depending on his or her stage of development, you might wish to further your child's understanding of the alphabet by working with crayon or pencil and paper after completing an activity. But don't feel that you must follow the letters of the alphabet in sequence. You need not start at A and work through to Z to provide the best learning experience. Skip around as you like, according to the moods and tastes of you both. Also, you do not need to engage in every activity that accompanies each recipe. You may prefer to develop some activities of your own.

Some of the recipes specify cooking or baking time, so perhaps you'll want to help develop time concepts with the child. You can do this by indicating where the minute hand (or to the child, the "large" or "big" hand) on a clock will be at a certain time and have him or her observe and let you know. You might mark the point with a crayon or grease pencil to help the child. You might set a timer, or teach the child to do so. Or you might use both methods together.

This book suggests ways to help your child develop learning skills, as well as opportunities for you and your child to have fun together while preparing food and eating it. So relax and enjoy yourself.

# A is for Applesauce

## EQUIPMENT

Blender                    Teaspoon measure
Measuring cup              2 plates
Knife

## RECIPE

4 apples
¼ cup water or apple juice
¼ cup sugar
⅛ teaspoon cinnamon (or substitute ¼ cup cinnamon candy
    for cinnamon and sugar)
A few drops ascorbic acid

Peel, quarter, and core apples. Place water or apple juice and
ascorbic acid in blender. Cover and process at *puree* until
smooth. Stop blender, remove cap, and with appliance at
*blend* add remaining pieces of apple, a few at a time.
Add sugar and cinnamon or cinnamon candy as the mixing
progresses.

# Activities

1. Review with the child the names of all the equipment and
   ingredients, pointing to each: blender, measuring cup, knife,
   teaspoon measure, plates, water or apple juice, apples, sugar,
   cinnamon (or cinnamon candy), ascorbic acid.

2. Suggest that the child dip a finger in the sugar and cinnamon and
   taste the ingredients, describing the taste. The word "sweet"
   will come readily to mind, but you might have to work a bit to
   get a word describing the cinnamon taste. Encourage the child
   to make up a word if he or she wishes.

3. Have the child count the apples—help if necessary. Then divide
   them into groups of one and three. Ask the child to count
   those in the first group (one), then in the other (three). Ask,

"How many apples are there all together?" Say, "One and three make _____ ." Divide the apples into groups of two each. Ask, "Now how many are there in each group?" "And altogether?" "So two and two also make _____ ." Noting that there are two apples in each group, suggest the idea of equality. Then make comparisons with other objects in groups of twos in the room.

4. Ask the child, "What color are the apples?" (They might be red, green, or yellow.) With the color established ask, "Can you find other things in the kitchen that are the same color as the apples?"

5. Allow the child to try peeling the apples, if you think he or she is capable. You may need to finish the task yourself.

6. Place one of the apples on the counter before the child. Guiding him or her, have the child cut the apple in half (approximately will do). Say, "We have cut the apple in the middle to make two pieces. Are the two pieces the same size or different?" (The concept of equality again.) Introduce the words "half" and "two halves." Have the child reassemble the two pieces to make a whole. Point out what he or she has done.

7. Say, "We will now divide each of these pieces in the middle." Now ask, "Is each piece the same size?" (The concept of equality once more.) Count the pieces with the child and discuss how two go together to make a half, all four to make a whole, having the child reassemble them as proof. Now, quarter the remaining apples.

8. Have the child, if he or she can manage it, remove the core of the apple pieces.

9. Have the child operate the blender buttons. Guide him or her by referring to the proper ones by color or, if they are not colored, by pointing to them. Have the child place four pieces of apple in the blender, and measure and add the water or apple juice and the ascorbic acid. Once the initial blending is completed, have him or her add the remaining pieces and measure and add the sugar and cinnamon or cinnamon candy. As the child adds the pieces of apple, ask him or her to practice counting.

10. When the applesauce is ready, serve it on plates in this manner: spoon out the sauce to form the letter *A* on one plate. Say, "This is the letter *A*. It is the first letter in the word *applesauce*."

Then have the child spoon out applesauce in the same way to form an *A* on the other plate.

11. As you and the child sample the applesauce, discuss the activities, having the child recall the steps of preparation in sequence. If necessary, assist by asking such questions as "What did we do next?" "Then what did we do?"

# Skills

## MOTOR
- peeling
- cutting
- measuring and pouring ingredients
- forming the letter A

## LANGUAGE
- naming equipment and ingredients
- using number words
- naming colors
- naming the letter A
- describing tastes
- relating the sequence of activities to prepare recipe

## COGNITIVE
- counting
- measuring ingredients
- recognizing equal sets
- recognizing fractional parts; quarter, half, and whole
- identifying colors and objects of similar colors
- recognizing tastes and foods having similar tastes
- reviewing the sequence of activities

# B *is for* Butter

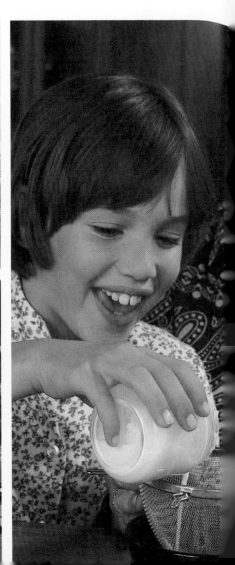

## EQUIPMENT

Container with tight-fitting lid
   (example: Mason jar)      Toaster
Scraper                    Plate
Fine sieve               Knife
Bowl                     Spoon

## RECIPE

½ pint whipping cream
  2–4 slices bread

Pour the whipping cream into a container with tight-fitting lid. Shake vigorously until butter forms. Pour contents through sieve. Pat the solids remaining in the sieve into shape and lift onto plate. Spread butter on toasted bread.

# Activities

1. Review with the child the names of all the equipment and ingredients, pointing to each: container (jar), scraper, spoon, sieve, bowl, toaster, knife, plate, whipping cream, bread.

2. Have the child open the carton of whipping cream and pour the cream into the container, closing its lid tightly (you'll want to check this). Then have the child shake the container ten times, with both of you counting. If the child is not yet able to count to ten, count with him or her as far as possible and complete the count yourself.

3. Remove the lid—you might have to do this yourself if it is tight— and check the results. Discuss the change that is taking place. (If you use a clear jar you can, of course, check the results without removing the lid.) Replace the lid and have the child continue shaking the jar, while you both count, until butter forms.

4. Remove the lid and have the child pour the contents through the sieve into the bowl.

5. Ask, "Why does some of the contents pass through the tiny holes, and some remain in the sieve?" Here, talk about the concepts of solid and liquid, although you might wish to use other terms (butter—like paste, liquid—like water).

6. Have the child use the scraper to pat the butter into shape in the sieve. Then have him or her remove the butter with a spoon and place it on a plate.

7. Have the child insert two bread slices into the toaster and push the lever.

8. When the toast is ready, use the tip of a knife to scrape the form of the letter *B* on one slice. Say, "This is the letter *B*. It is the first letter in the word *butter*." Have the child scrape the other piece of toast, assisting him or her if necessary.

9. Then have the child spread the butter over the letter *B* on both pieces of toast, again assisting if necessary.

10. While munching the toast (with jam or jelly if you like), discuss the activities, having the child recall the steps of preparation in sequence. If necessary, assist by asking such questions as "What did we do next?" "Then what did we do?"

# Skills

## MOTOR
- shaking container (jar)
- opening cream carton
- pouring liquid
- fastening and unfastening lid
- manipulating scraper, spoon, and knife
- pushing toaster lever
- making the letter B

## LANGUAGE
- naming equipment and ingredients
- using number words
- naming the letter B
- relating sequence of activities to prepare recipe

## COGNITIVE
- counting
- recognizing solid and liquid
- reviewing the sequence of activities

# C is for Cocoa

**EQUIPMENT**

2 mugs (cups)
  Spoon

**RECIPE**

2 packages cocoa mix
2 cups hot water
  Miniature marshmallows

Pour contents of cocoa packages into mugs. Fill with hot water and stir. Add marshmallows.

# Activities

1. Review with the child the names of all the equipment and ingredients, pointing to each: cocoa, mugs (cups), spoon, water, marshmallows.

2. Have the child open the cocoa mix packages and pour the contents into the mugs.

3. Assisting if necessary, have the child fill the mugs with hot water from the tap. (Hot water from the tap is safe to use and hot enough for cocoa. The mixture is ready to drink sooner than it would be with boiling water, although an adult might prefer to use the latter.) Have the child stir the mixture.

4. Place some marshmallows on the counter, the child assisting. Then, using whatever number necessary, form the letter *C* on the counter with them. Say, "This is the letter *C*. It is the first letter in the word *cocoa*." Have the child use marshmallows to form the letter.

5. Have the child put marshmallows into the mugs of hot cocoa, one at a time, counting each. Assist with the count if necessary.

6. As you sip the cocoa, discuss the activities, having the child recall the steps of preparation in sequence. If necessary, assist by asking such questions as "What did we do next?" "Then what did we do?"

# Skills

## MOTOR
- opening and emptying packages
- grasping mug (cup)
- stirring
- arranging marshmallows to form the letter C

## LANGUAGE
- naming equipment and ingredients
- using number words
- naming the letter C
- relating sequence of activities to prepare recipe

## COGNITIVE
- counting
- reviewing the sequence of activities

# D is for Doughnuts

## EQUIPMENT

Tablespoon measure          Plate
½ cup measure               Spoon
Pastry brush                Pastry board
Deep saucepan               Paper towels
Tongs                       D-shaped cookie cutter

(If you cannot obtain cookie cutter locally, letter cookie cutters are available from Wilton Enterprises, Inc., 833 West 115th Street, Chicago, Illinois, 60643.)

## RECIPE

1 large-sized can refrigerated biscuits
  Shortening or cooking oil
  Flour
  Glaze: ½ cup powdered sugar
         1 tablespoon milk

Open refrigerated biscuits, sprinkle flour on pastry board, and spread dough—pushing all the biscuits together. Cut with D-shaped cookie cutter, then fry quickly in oil or shortening at 350° to 400°. Remove with tongs and place on paper towels to drain. Combine glaze ingredients and spread glaze on doughnuts with pastry brush.

# Activities

1. Review with the child the names of all the equipment and ingredients, pointing to each: tablespoon measure, one-half cup measure, pastry board, pastry brush, saucepan, tongs, plate, spoon, paper towels, cookie cutter, refrigerated biscuits, shortening (cooking oil), flour, powdered sugar, milk.

2. Begin heating the cooking oil or shortening.

3. If the child can manage it, have him or her open the can of biscuits and separate them. Then count the biscuits with the child, finishing the count yourself if necessary.

4. Have the child sprinkle flour on the pastry board and lay out the dough, pushing the biscuits together and patting them down.

5. Show the cookie cutter to the child. Say, "This makes the letter *D*. That is the first letter in the word *doughnut*." Demonstrate by cutting out a doughnut. Then say, "Now you use the cutter and make more letters." Once they are all cut, count them with the child, again encouraging him or her to count as far as possible.

6. Unless the child is particularly adept, it is probably best for you to place the doughnuts in the oil or shortening. Either you or the child might remove them when they are cooked sufficiently. Practice counting again as the doughnuts are placed on the paper towels to drain.

7. Have the child measure the ingredients for the glaze and stir the mixture. Then have him or her use the pastry brush to cover the doughnuts with glaze.

8. As the two of you enjoy the doughnuts, perhaps with milk, discuss the activities, having the child recall the steps of preparation in sequence. If necessary, assist by asking such questions as "What did we do next?" "Then what did we do?"

# Skills

## MOTOR
- sprinkling flour
- peeling paper from can of biscuits
- breaking open can of biscuits
- separating biscuits and patting dough together on pastry board
- using the cookie cutter
- measuring and pouring ingredients
- spreading glaze

## LANGUAGE
- naming equipment and ingredients
- using number words
- naming the letter D
- relating the sequence of activities to prepare recipe

## COGNITIVE
- counting
- measuring ingredients
- reviewing the sequence of activities

# E *is for*
# English Toffee

## EQUIPMENT

Saucepan
Cup measure
Tablespoon measure
Wooden spoon
Teaspoon measure

Candy thermometer
9" x 9" baking pan
Knife
Crayon or grease pencil

## RECIPE

1 cup sugar
2 sticks margarine
   Shortening or cooking oil
3 tablespoons water
1 teaspoon vanilla
7 chocolate candy bars, about 4 inches long, or 1 small bag of chocolate chips
¼ cup finely chopped pecans

Combine sugar, margarine, and water; cook to 300°, testing with candy thermometer, stirring constantly. Add vanilla, stir, and pour mixture into greased 9" x 9" pan. Lay chocolate bars or chips on top and spread evenly as they melt. While the chocolate is still warm, sprinkle pecans over top. Cool thoroughly, then break toffee into pieces.

# Activities

1. Review with the child the names of all the equipment and ingredients, pointing to each: cup measure, wooden spoon, tablespoon measure, teaspoon measure, candy thermometer, baking pan, shortening (cooking oil), knife, saucepan, sugar, margarine, vanilla, candy bars or chocolate chips, pecans, crayon or grease pencil.

2. Discuss the colors of the sugar, margarine, candy bars, and pecans. Ask the child to locate objects with similar colors in the room.

3. Have the child grease the 9″ x 9″ pan with shortening or cooking oil. Explain to him or her that this is done so that the toffee will not stick to the pan.

4. Ask the child to unwrap the two sticks of margarine and place them in the saucepan, counting each. Have him or her measure one cup of sugar and empty it into the pan, then measure and add three tablespoons of water, counting each. Place the pan on the burner and have the child stir the mixture with the wooden spoon as it heats.

5. Show the child the red line on the candy thememometer and the 300° line. You may want to mark the degree line with a crayon or grease pencil so that it will be more easily seen. Say, "Watch the red line go up. When it gets to here, the 300° line, the candy will be done." As the child stirs, add the vanilla. Talk about its smell and ask the child to suggest things that have a similar smell. Once the mixture reaches the proper temperature, pour it into the greased 9″ x 9″ pan. Or have the child pour, depending on his or her skill.

6. Now ask the child to unwrap the candy bars, or open the bag of chocolate chips. Place the chocolate over the candy mixture in the pan in the shape of the letter *E*.

7. Say, "This is what the letter *E* looks like. It is the first letter in the word *English,* as in *English toffee.*"

8. Hand the knife to the child and ask him or her to spread the melting chocolate *E* over the top of the candy.

9. Now have the child use the chopped nuts to form the *E* again. If necessary, remind him or her where each line goes, using the words left, top, bottom, and between.

10. As you munch the candy, discuss the activities, having the child recall the steps of preparation in sequence. If necessary, assist by asking such questions as "What did we do next?" "Then what did we do?"

# Skills

## MOTOR

- stirring
- making the letter E
- greasing pan
- measuring and pouring ingredients
- unwrapping margarine and candy bars or chocolate chips
- arranging candy bars or chocolate chips
- sprinkling pecans

## LANGUAGE

- naming equipment and ingredients
- naming colors
- using number words
- describing the smell of vanilla and items with a similar smell
- naming the letter E
- relating the sequence of activities to prepare recipe

## COGNITIVE

- identifying colors and objects of similar colors
- recognizing positions; left, top, bottom, between
- counting
- measuring ingredients and temperature
- recognizing the smell of vanilla and items having a similar smell
- reviewing the sequence of activities

# F is for Fudge

## EQUIPMENT

Cup measure                 Pastry board
¼-cup measure               Mixing bowl
Wooden spoon                Waxed paper
Sifter

## RECIPE

    1 cup peanut butter
    1 cup corn syrup
1¼ cup dry milk
1¼ cup powdered sugar, sifted
    ¼ cup cocoa
        Nuts (optional)

Blend peanut butter and corn syrup in large mixing bowl; add
dry milk and one cup sifted powdered sugar (the additional
one-fourth cup will be used later). Add cocoa. Mix with
wooden spoon, then knead ingredients on pastry board
lightly covered with one-fourth cup sifted powdered sugar
until smooth. Top with nuts if desired.

# Activities

1. Review with the child the names of all the equipment and
   ingredients, pointing to each: cup measure, one-fourth cup
   measure, wooden spoon, pastry board, mixing bowl, waxed paper,
   sifter, peanut butter, corn syrup, dry milk, powdered sugar, cocoa,
   nuts (optional).

2. Discuss the colors and tastes of the peanut butter, corn syrup,
   cocoa, dry milk, and powdered sugar. Ask the child to name items
   of similar tastes and locate objects of similar colors in the room.

3. Have the child measure one cup of peanut butter into the mixing
   bowl, followed by the cup of corn syrup.

4. Next, have him or her measure the dry milk (using the one-cup and the one-fourth cup) and add it to the mixture. Have him or her measure and sift one cup of powdered sugar into the bowl, then measure and add the cocoa. The child can now stir the mixture with the wooden spoon.

5. Now have him or her sift one-fourth cup of powdered sugar over the pastry board and place the fudge on it. Demonstrate how to knead the mixture, using the fingers to pull it from the top and the heels of the hands to push it away, picking up and mixing in more powdered sugar in the process. Have the child complete the kneading.

6. Using the tip of a spoon, draw a large *F* on the waxed paper. Divide the candy mixture in half. Give one piece to the child, and have him or her roll and stretch it into a strip about as long as the vertical line on the *F* . Then have the child place the strip over the line drawn on the paper. Divide the remaining candy into two equal parts and have the child repeat the rolling and stretching process with each piece. Finally, have the child position the strips to complete the letter. Say, "This is the letter *F*. It is the first letter in the word *fudge*." If nuts are used, have the child sprinkle them over the fudge.

7. As you sample the fudge, discuss the activities, having the child recall the steps of preparation in sequence. If necessary, assist by asking such questions as "What did we do next?" "Then what did we do?"

# Skills

## MOTOR
- stirring
- sifting
- kneading
- measuring and pouring ingredients
- opening and closing boxes and jars
- rolling and stretching candy
- forming the letter F

## LANGUAGE
- naming equipment and ingredients
- naming colors
- describing tastes
- naming the letter F
- relating the sequence of activities to prepare recipe

## COGNITIVE
- identifying colors and objects of similar colors.
- recognizing tastes and foods having similar tastes
- measuring ingredients
- reviewing the sequence of activities

# G is for Gingerbread Man

## EQUIPMENT

Tablespoon measure
Gingerbread man cookie cutter
Large mixing bowl
Wooden spoon

Pastry cloth
Sifter
Rolling pin
Cookie sheet

## RECIPE

1 box gingerbread mix
3 rounded tablespoons powdered sugar
4 tablespoons orange or lemon juice
   Shortening or cooking oil
   Flour

Sift gingerbread mix and sugar into mixing bowl. Add the juice and stir until moist. Form into a ball and roll out on floured pastry board to one-eighth inch thickness. Cut with floured gingerbread man cutter. Place on a greased cookie sheet and bake at 350° for ten to twelve minutes.

# Activities

1. Review with the child the names of all the equipment and ingredients, pointing to each: tablespoon measure, gingerbread man cutter, mixing bowl, sifter, wooden spoon, pastry cloth, rolling pin, cookie sheet, gingerbread mix, powdered sugar, orange or lemon juice, flour, shortening (cooking oil).

2. Discuss the colors and tastes of the gingerbread mix, powdered sugar, and orange or lemon juice. Ask the child to suggest items of similar tastes, and locate objects of similar colors in the room. Have the child rub a little cooking oil or shortening between a thumb and forefinger and describe the "greasy" or "oily" feeling.

3. Have the child grease the cookie sheet with shortening or cooking oil. Explain that this is done so that the gingerbread men will not stick to the sheet.

4. Have the child open the box of gingerbread mix. Then have him or her measure the powdered sugar into the sifter, add the mix, and sift into the bowl. Next have the child measure and add the juice, the two of you counting each spoonful together. The child can now stir the mixture with the wooden spoon.

5. When ingredients are thoroughly mixed, have him or her form the dough into a ball by pressing it together with the hands.

6. Have the child flour the pastry cloth, place the ball on it, and roll out the ball with the rolling pin until the dough is about one-eighth inch thick.

7. Next have him or her dip the gingerbread man cutter into flour and cut out the shapes from the dough.

8. As the cutting progresses, discuss the body parts: "Where is the gingerbread man's head?" Repeat the question for the neck, arms, chest, legs, feet.

9. Let the child place the forms on the greased cookie sheet, counting each. When the child can count no further, you may continue until all are counted. Bake at 350° for ten to twelve minutes.

10. As the gingerbread men bake, have the child gather the leftover dough and form it into a strip. Then have him or her tear off a short piece. With the longer piece, help the child shape three-quarters of a circle. Finally, have him or her put the shorter piece in place to form the letter G. Say, "This is the letter G. It is the first letter in the word *gingerbread,* as in *gingerbread man.*"

11. As you and the child snack, discuss the activities, having the child recall the steps of preparation in sequence. If necessary, assist by asking questions as "What did we do next?" "Then what did we do?"

# Skills

## MOTOR

- stirring
- sifting
- using rolling pin
- greasing cookie sheet
- measuring and pouring ingredients
- opening and closing containers
- forming dough into a ball
- sprinkling flour on pastry board
- using gingerbread man cutter
- forming the letter G

## LANGUAGE

- naming equipment and ingredients
- using number words
- naming colors
- describing tastes
- naming parts of the body
- naming the letter G
- relating the sequence of activities to prepare recipe

## COGNITIVE

- identifying colors and objects of similar colors
- recognizing tastes and foods having similar tastes
- recognizing an oily or greasy texture
- counting
- measuring ingredients
- identifying parts of the body
- reviewing the sequence of activities

# H is for Hotcakes

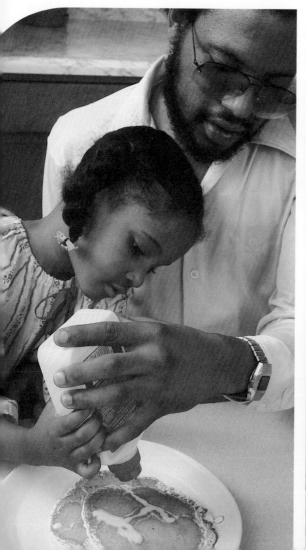

## EQUIPMENT

Griddle                     Large spoon
Mixing bowl                 Tablespoon measure
Cup measure                 Spatula
½-teaspoon measure          Paper towel or napkin
Wire whisk                  Teaspoon measure

## RECIPE

1 cup flour
2 heaping teaspoons baking powder
½ teaspoon salt
1 cup milk
1 egg
3 tablespoons cooking oil
  Squeeze margarine
  Syrup

Combine the first six ingredients in mixing bowl in order
listed, folding in gently. Mix with wire whisk, but do not
remove all lumps. Spoon pancakes of desired size on lightly
greased, heated griddle. Bake until the tops are covered with
bubbles, then turn and bake other side.

# Activities

1. Review with the child the names of all the equipment and
   ingredients, pointing to each: griddle, mixing bowl, cup measure,
   one-half teaspoon measure, whisk, spoon, tablespoon measure,
   teaspoon measure, spatula, squeeze margarine, paper towel or
   napkin, flour, baking powder, salt, milk, egg, cooking oil, syrup.

2. Discuss with the child the colors and tastes of the margarine, flour,
   baking powder, salt, and milk. Ask the child to suggest items
   having similar tastes, and locate objects of similar colors in the
   room. Have the child rub a little cooking oil between a thumb and
   forefinger and describe the "oily" feeling.

3. Have the child open the bottle of cooking oil and pour a small amount of oil on the griddle, spreading it around with a paper towel or napkin. Explain that this is done so that the pancakes will not stick to the griddle.

4. Next, have the child measure and pour the flour, baking powder, salt, and milk into the bowl. If the child can manage it, let him or her crack the egg on the side of the bowl and add it to the mixture. You might also discuss the white and the yolk, noting their colors, and ask the child to identify other objects of similar colors in the kitchen. Now have the child measure and add the cooking oil, counting each tablespoonful.

5. Show the child how to hold the wire whisk, whirling it back and forth between the palms of the hands. Then have him or her use the whisk to mix the ingredients.

6. Using a spoon, pour batter on the hot griddle in the shape of an *H*. Say, "This is the letter *H*. It is the first letter in the word *hotcakes*." Then cover the letter with additional batter to make the desired size of hotcake. Have the child form an *H* with batter and then cover it as you did. When the hotcakes are done on one side, if the child can manage it, have him or her use the spatula to turn them.

7. Once the hotcakes are ready, help the child remove them from the griddle to a plate, with the *H* up. Ask him or her to squeeze the margarine over the letter *H*.

8. Finally, have the child pour syrup over the hotcakes. They are now ready to eat.

9. Discuss the activities with the child, having him or her recall the steps of preparation in sequence. If necessary, assist by asking such questions as "What did we do next?" "Then what did we do?"

# Skills

## MOTOR

- removing and replacing cooking oil cap
- measuring and pouring ingredients
- greasing griddle
- twirling wire whisk
- spooning batter onto griddle
- turning hotcakes
- removing hotcakes
- squeezing margarine on the hotcakes
- forming the letter H

## LANGUAGE

- naming equipment and ingredients
- naming colors
- describing tastes
- using number words
- naming the letter H
- relating the sequence of activities to prepare recipe

## COGNITIVE

- identifying colors and objects of similar colors
- recognizing tastes and foods having similar tastes
- recognizing an oily texture
- counting
- measuring ingredients
- reviewing the sequence of activities.

# I is for Ice Cream

## EQUIPMENT

1-gallon ice cream freezer          Cup measure
  (hand or electric)          Tablespoon measure
Mixing bowl          Foil or waxed paper
Large spoon          Beater or electric mixer

## RECIPE

  6 eggs
  2 cups sugar
  1 can sweetened condensed milk
  1 tablespoon vanilla
½ gallon whole milk
  1 box ice cream salt
20 lbs. crushed ice

Beat eggs and sugar together but do not overbeat.
Add condensed milk and vanilla. Pour into one-gallon freezer
can with dasher in place. Finish filling with whole milk.
Put cover in place and add ice and salt around the outside.
Dash until frozen. Remove dasher and cover top with foil or
waxed paper before replacing lid. Pack with ice and let set
for one to three hours.

# Activities

1. Review with the child the names of all the equipment and
   ingredients: ice cream freezer, mixing bowl, spoon, beater or
   electric mixer, cup measure, tablespoon measure, foil or waxed
   paper, eggs, sugar, condensed milk, whole milk, vanilla, ice cream
   salt, ice.

2. Have the child measure the sugar and place it in the bowl, counting
   each cup.

3. If the child is able, have him or her crack the eggs and add them.
   Or demonstrate the process with the first one or two eggs and

45

have the child finish cracking the rest. You might discuss the whites and yolks and their colors. Ask the child to point to other objects of similar colors in the room.

4. Have the child turn on the mixer, indicating the appropriate button. Then have him or her open the can of condensed milk, add the milk to the mixture, and measure and add the vanilla. Discuss the smell of vanilla and ask the child to think of other substances that have a similar smell. You might also have the child taste the condensed milk and describe its sweet taste.

5. If the child can manage it, have him or her pour the mixture into the freezer can. Either you or the child can add the whole milk. Position the lid, place the can in the freezer bucket, and position the crank mechanism. Both of you pour salt into the bucket, alternating with ice and salt until the can is completely covered. At the same time, have the child feel a handful of salt and describe its rough texture. Ask him or her how the ice feels (cold, wet, smooth).

6. If you have a hand-cranked freezer, alternate turns with the child, each going ten to twenty times. When counting the turns, count with the child as far as he or she can go, completing

the count yourself if necessary. Add more ice and salt as needed. As the ice cream grows firmer, you will probably have to take over the turning process.

7. Frost will form on the outside of the freezer can. Using your fingernail, or a knife or some other tool, scrape the letter *I* in the frost. Say, "This is the letter *I*. It is the first letter of the word *ice*, as in *ice cream*." Encourage the child to draw more *I*'s in the frost.

8. As you both enjoy the ice cream, discuss the activities, having the child recall the steps of preparation in sequence. If necessary, assist by asking such questions as "What did we do next?" "Then what did we do?"

# Skills

## MOTOR
- turning freezer crank
- measuring and pouring ingredients
- cracking eggs and adding contents to the mixture
- pouring mixture and milk into the freezer container
- placing salt and ice in the freezer bucket
- making the letter I

## LANGUAGE
- naming equipment and ingredients
- using number words
- describing the smell of vanilla
- describing tastes
- describing textures
- naming the letter I
- relating the sequence of activities to prepare recipe

## COGNITIVE
- identifying colors and objects of similar colors
- recognizing tastes and foods having similar tastes
- recognizing the smell of vanilla and items having a similar smell
- counting
- measuring ingredients
- identifying textures and temperatures: rough, cold, wet, smooth
- reviewing the sequence of activities

# J is for Jell-o

## EQUIPMENT

Pint jar with lid
Crayon or grease pencil

## RECIPE

3-ounce box Jell-O
Hot water
Tray of ice cubes

Follow the directions on the Jell-O box.

# Activities

1. Review with the child the names of all the equipment and ingredients, pointing to each: jar, crayon or grease pencil, Jell-O, hot water, ice cubes.

2. Ask the child to open the box of Jell-O, assisting if necessary.

3. Have him or her dip a finger into the Jell-O, taste it and describe the "tart" sensation. Ask the child to identify the fruit flavor and color, referring to the color or picture of fruit on the box. Have the child locate other objects in the kitchen that have a color similar to the Jell-O.

4. Have the child remove the lid from the jar and pour the Jell-O into it. Then draw a line with the crayon or grease pencil at the half-way point on the jar. Say, "Now run hot water from the tap into the jar until the water comes up to this line—half-full."

5. Have him or her place a hand or a finger on the outside bottom of the jar and describe the sensation (warm or hot). Then have the child touch the outside top portion and describe the feeling (cool or cold).

6. Now ask the child to replace the cover on the jar—check to see that it is tight—and have him or her shake the jar vigorously until the mixture is dissolved.

7. Have the child once more remove the lid—assisting if necessary—and add ice cubes until the jar is full. Both of you count the cubes as they are added. Allow the child to count as far as he or she can, then continue counting yourself until all are counted.

8. Replace the lid and have the child once again shake the jar until the ice has melted. Note with the child that the warmer liquid has helped change the ice (a solid) into water (a liquid). Observe with the child that the jar is now cold all over.

9. Now have the child place the jar in the refrigerator so the Jell-O will set.

10. Once the Jell-O is ready, have the child remove the jar and note the condensation that forms on the outside of the jar when it comes in contact with warmer air. Place the jar on the counter and, taking the forefinger of the child's dominant hand (the one

used for eating), help him or her draw the letter *J* in the condensation. Then have the child do it alone. Say, "This is the letter *J*. It is the first letter in the word *Jell-O*."

11. As you eat the Jell-O, discuss the activities, having the child recall the events of preparation in sequence. If necessary, assist by asking such questions as "What did we do next?" "Then what did we do?"

# Skills

## MOTOR
- shaking jar
- opening Jell-O box
- pouring
- removing and replacing jar lid
- placing ice cubes in the jar
- using forefinger to draw the letter J

## LANGUAGE
- naming the equipment and ingredients
- describing the Jell-O flavor and color
- describing temperatures: warm, hot, cool, cold
- using number words
- naming the letter J
- relating the sequence of activities to prepare recipe

## COGNITIVE
- recognizing taste
- counting
- identifying colors and objects of similar colors
- recognizing fractional parts: half-full, full
- recognizing temperatures: warm, hot, cool, cold
- recognizing solid and liquid
- reviewing the sequence of activities

# K is for Kisses

## EQUIPMENT

Large mixing bowl
Beater or electric mixer
Cup measure
Tablespoon measure
Teaspoon measure

Wooden spoon
Teaspoon
Cookie sheet
Egg separator (optional)

## RECIPE

2 egg whites
1 cup light brown sugar
2 tablespoons flour
1 teaspoon vanilla
2 cups chopped nuts
   Shortening or cooking oil

Beat egg whites until stiff, gradually adding brown sugar and flour. Add vanilla and fold in nuts. Drop by teaspoonfuls, allowing space for expansion, on greased cookie sheet. Bake at 250° thirty-five to forty minutes.

# Activities

1. Review with the child the names of all the equipment and ingredients, pointing to each: mixing bowl, beater or electric mixer, cup measure, tablespoon measure, teaspoon measure, wooden spoon, teaspoon, cookie sheet, egg separator (optional), eggs, brown sugar, flour, vanilla, chopped nuts, shortening (cooking oil).

2. Discuss the colors and tastes of the brown sugar and flour and see if the child can suggest items with similar tastes. Ask the child to name objects of similar colors in the room. Have the child rub a little shortening or cooking oil between a thumb and forefinger and describe the "greasy" or "oily" feeling.

3. Count the eggs with the child. Then crack one and demonstrate the egg separator—or separate by pouring from one half of shell into the other. Place the whites in the mixing bowl and the yolks in a jar or cup for later use. Then have the child go through the procedure. Discuss the colors of whites and yolks and have the child find other objects of similar colors in the room.

4. If you use a hand beater, demonstrate how it is used and then have the child beat the eggs (you might have to finish the beating yourself). If you use an electric mixer, have the child turn it on and off at your direction.

5. Either you or the child measure and add the brown sugar and the flour, counting the tablespoonfuls. As the vanilla is added, discuss its smell with the child, and see if he or she can name similiar smells.

6. Finally, have the child measure and count the two cups of nuts, and add them to the mixture.

7. Using shortening or cooking oil, grease a portion of the cookie sheet in the shape of a large *K*, the length and width of the sheet. Explain that this is done to prevent the kisses from sticking to the sheet.

8. Show the child how to drop the batter by teaspoonfuls onto the greased portion of the sheet. Then let him or her finish the rest. Count the kisses as they are laid out. Count with the child as far as he or she can go, completing the count yourself if necessary.

9. After all the batter has been dropped, point out to the child: "This is the letter *K*. It is the first letter in the word *kisses*." Now bake at 250° for thirty-five to forty minutes. (Have the child grease the *K* in subsequent batches.)

10. As the kisses bake, or while you eat them, discuss the activities, having the child recall the events of preparation in sequence. If necessary, assist by asking such questions as "What did we do next?" "Then what did we do?"

# Skills

## MOTOR
- beating egg whites (if hand beater is used)
- measuring and pouring ingredients
- cracking and separating eggs
- grasping hand beater
- dropping batter on cookie sheet
- greasing the letter K on cookie sheet

## LANGUAGE
- naming equipment and ingredients
- describing the smell of vanilla
- using number words
- naming colors
- describing tastes
- naming the letter K
- relating the sequence of activities to prepare recipe

## COGNITIVE
- identifying colors and objects of similar colors
- recognizing tastes and foods having similar tastes
- recognizing a greasy or oily texture
- recognizing the smell of vanilla and items having a similar smell
- counting
- measuring ingredients
- reviewing the sequence of activities

# L *is for* Lemonade

## EQUIPMENT

2 drinking glasses
Juice squeezer (hand)
Tablespoon measure

Spoon
Bendable straws

## RECIPE

2 lemons, halved
2 tablespoons sugar (more if desired)
   Ice cubes

Halve lemons, squeeze them, and pour the juice of one into each glass. Add sugar and stir until dissolved, then add water and ice.

# Activities

1. Review with the child the names of all the equipment and ingredients, pointing to each: drinking glasses, juice squeezer, tablespoon measure, spoon, straws, lemons, sugar, ice cubes.

2. Count the lemons with the child and discuss the color. Ask the child to find objects of similar color in the kitchen.

3. If the child can manage it, have him or her cut the lemons in half. Referring to the two halves ask, "How many pieces do we have? Each one is called a ___ (half). Now put the two together to make a whole lemon. How many halves make a whole lemon?"

4. Have the child taste the lemon. Discuss the "sour" sensation, comparing it to the taste of sugar. Ask the child to think of other things that taste like the lemon.

5. If necessary, demonstrate how to use the juice squeezer. Then have the child try to squeeze the lemon halves (complete it yourself if necessary). Once one lemon has been squeezed, have the child pour its juice into the first glass. Then have him or her pour juice from the other lemon into the second glass.

6. Have the child measure and add the sugar, stirring the mixture until the sugar is dissolved. Then have him or her run cold water from the tap into the glasses until each is half-full. Discuss "half-full," contrasting it with "full," which the glasses become as the child adds ice cubes. Count the cubes with the child as he or she adds them, completing the count yourself if necessary.

7. Take a straw and hold it upright in front of the child. Then bend the straw toward his or her right. Say, "This is the letter *L*. It is the first letter in the words *lemon* and *lemonade*." Have the child form the letter with other straws.

8. As you drink the lemonade, discuss the activities, having the child recall the events of preparation in sequence. If necessary, assist by asking such questions as "What did we do next?" "Then what did we do?"

# Skills

## MOTOR

- cutting lemon
- squeezing lemon
- measuring and pouring ingredients
- stirring
- adding ice cubes
- bending straws to make the letter L

## LANGUAGE

- naming equipment and ingredients
- naming the color yellow
- describing sweet and sour tastes
- using number words
- naming the letter L
- relating sequence of activities to prepare recipe

## COGNITIVE

- identifying the color yellow and objects of similar color
- recognizing and comparing sweet and sour tastes
- counting
- recognizing fractional parts: half, whole, half-full, full
- reviewing the sequence of activities

# M is for Marshmallow Candy

## EQUIPMENT

| | | |
|---|---|---|
| Sifter | Cup measure | 15" x 10" baking pan |
| Double boiler | ⅓-cup measure | Beater or electric mixer |
| Brown paper | Teaspoon measure | M-shaped cookie cutter |
| Waxed paper | Wooden spoon | Egg separator (optional) |
| Pastry brush | 2-quart saucepan | |

(If cookie cutter is not available locally, letter-shaped cookie cutters can be obtained from Wilton Enterprises, Inc., 833 West 115th Street, Chicago, Illinois, 60643.)

## RECIPE

| | |
|---|---|
| 1 cup sugar | Powdered sugar |
| 1 cup light corn syrup | 1 12-ounce package |
| ⅓ cup water | semi-sweet |
| 2 envelopes unflavored gelatin | chocolate pieces |
| 1 teaspoon vanilla | Decorative candies |
| 1 egg white | (optional) |

In two-quart saucepan mix sugar, corn syrup, and water. Cook at medium heat and stir until sugar dissolves. Then cook without stirring to soft ball stage. Stir in gelatin and vanilla. Cool ten minutes. Then gradually add mixture to stiffly beaten egg white. Line pan with brown paper, spread candy into pan and let stand, uncovered, overnight.

Sift powdered sugar over a second sheet of brown paper. Invert pan. The original paper is now on top. Moisten it with water, using pastry brush. Peel off paper. Cut out shapes, using the M-shaped cookie cutter.

In small double boiler, melt chocolate pieces, stirring constantly. Using a pastry brush, brush chocolate over candy shapes. Place on waxed paper and sprinkle with small colored decorative candies, if desired.

# Activities

1. Review with the child the names of all the equipment and ingredients, pointing to each.

2. Discuss the colors and tastes of the sugars, corn syrup, and chocolate pieces, and see if the child can suggest items with similar tastes.

3. Have the child measure sugar, corn syrup, and water and pour each into saucepan. Have the child stir mixture with wooden spoon until sugar dissolves. Ask the child to taste the sugar and corn syrup, compare them, and name other items that are sweet.

4. Have the child open the envelopes of gelatin and, counting the packages, add their contents to the mixture. Now have him or her measure and add the vanilla. Discuss the smell of vanilla and ask the child if he or she knows of other items that have similar smells. Have the child stir the mixture with the wooden spoon until it reaches the soft ball stage.

5. As the mixture cools, have the child crack and separate the egg. An egg separator may be used, or the method of pouring from one half of shell into the other. Discuss the colors of the egg and have the child find objects of similar colors in the kitchen.

6. If you use a hand beater, demonstrate its operation and handling to the child and have him or her try it. If you use an electric mixer, have the child push the appropriate buttons. Tell him or her to observe the beating process carefully; point out the peaks as they appear, a signal that the white has been whipped enough. When finished, have the child add the mixture to the egg white and stir with the wooden spoon. Then he or she can line the pan with brown paper and spread the candy in the pan to set overnight.

7. Demonstrate the use of the sifter, and have the child sift powdered sugar over the remaining piece of brown paper. Now invert the pan containing the candy on the paper—or have the child do this. Have the child use the pastry brush to spread cold water over the original paper. Have him or her peel the paper off.

8. Call the child's attention to the M-shaped cookie cutter and say, "This is the letter *M*. It is the first letter in the word *marsh-mallow,* as in *marshmallow candy.*" Dip the cookie cutter in cold water and cut out a letter. Then hand the cutter to the child and have him or her begin to cut out M-shapes. Then have the child count the pieces. Complete the counting yourself, if necessary.

9. Have the child open the package of chocolate pieces and place them in the double boiler. When the chocolate has melted, have the child brush chocolate on the M-shaped candies. Finally, have him or her sprinkle decorative candies over the chocolate if you wish to add them.

10. As you enjoy the marshmallow candy, discuss the activities, having the child recall the steps of preparation in sequence.

# Skills

## MOTOR
- operating hand beater
- stirring
- spreading candy in pan
- sifting, measuring and pouring ingredients
- cracking and separating egg
- opening packages
- placing chocolate pieces in boiler
- cutting candy forms
- using pastry brush
- spooning chocolate on candy
- sprinkling decorative candies

## LANGUAGE
- naming equipment and ingredients
- using number words
- naming colors
- describing tastes
- describing the vanilla smell
- naming the letter M
- relating sequence of activities to prepare recipe

## COGNITIVE
- identifying colors and objects of similar color
- recognizing and comparing tastes and foods having similar tastes
- counting
- measuring ingredients
- recognizing vanilla smell and items having a similar smell
- reviewing the sequence of activities

# N is for No-Bake Nuggets

## EQUIPMENT

Cup measure
½-cup measure
Rolling pin
Teaspoon

Waxed paper
Saucepan
Wooden spoon

## RECIPE

1 stick margarine
1 cup sugar
½ cup condensed milk
10 large marshmallows
1 cup crushed graham crackers
1 cup chopped nuts

Combine margarine, sugar, and milk; cook for six minutes, stirring constantly. Stir in remaining ingredients.
Drop in small balls onto waxed paper.

# Activities

1. Review with the child the names of all the equipment and ingredients, pointing to each: cup measure, one-half cup measure, rolling pin, waxed paper, saucepan, wooden spoon, teaspoon, margarine, sugar, condensed milk, marshmallows, crushed graham crackers, nuts.

2. Have the child unwrap the stick of margarine and place it in the saucepan.

3. Open the can of condensed milk, or have the child do it. Ask him or her to taste the milk and the sugar and compare the tastes. Now have the child measure the milk and sugar and pour them into the saucepan.

4. Have the child take a few graham crackers from the package. Count them together, completing the count yourself, if necessary.

Now have the child place the crackers between two sheets of waxed paper and crush them with the rolling pin.

5. Next, have him or her take ten marshmallows from the package, counting each one. Complete the count yourself, if necessary.

6. Discuss with the child the tastes and colors of the margarine, sugar, condensed milk, and graham crackers, and ask the child to suggest items with similar tastes, and name objects of similar colors in the room.

7. Have the child stir the mixture. When it has cooked for six minutes, remove it from the heat. Then have him or her add marshmallows one at a time, counting each one. Help with the count if necessary. Have the child measure the graham crackers and the nuts and stir them into the mixture.

8. Using the tip of a spoon, make an impression in the form of the letter *N* on a sheet of waxed paper. Then help the child use a teaspoon to drop balls of the mixture over the lines on the paper. When completed say, "This is the letter *N*. It is the first letter in the word *no*, as in *no-bake nuggets*." Count the nuggets with the child, and complete the count yourself if necessary.

9. As the no-bake nuggets melt in your mouths, discuss the activities, having the child recall the steps of preparation in sequence. If necessary, assist by asking such questions as "What did we do next?" "Then what did we do?"

# Skills

## MOTOR
- using rolling pin
- stirring
- unwrapping margarine
- opening condensed milk
- measuring and pouring ingredients
- removing graham crackers and marshmallows from packages
- dropping mixture by spoonfuls on waxed paper

## LANGUAGE
- naming equipment and ingredients
- using numbers
- naming colors
- describing tastes
- naming the letter N
- relating sequence of activities to prepare recipe

## COGNITIVE
- counting
- measuring ingredients
- identifying colors and objects of similar colors
- recognizing and comparing tastes and foods having similar tastes
- reviewing the sequence of activities

# O *is for* Oatmeal Drink

## EQUIPMENT

2 mugs (cups)                    Small saucepan
Blender                          Tablespoon measure
Cup measure

## RECIPE

2 cups hot milk
2 packets instant oatmeal, plain or spice-flavored
2 tablespoons honey

Heat milk in saucepan. Pour instant oatmeal into blender and
follow with milk and honey. Blend until smooth, then pour
into mugs.

# Activities

1. Review with the child the names of all the equipment and
   ingredients, pointing to each: mug (cup), blender, cup measure,
   saucepan, tablespoon measure, oatmeal, milk, honey.

2. Have the child measure and pour two cups of milk into the
   saucepan, counting each cup.

3. Then have him or her open the oatmeal packets and empty the
   contents into the blender. Have the child pour the milk into the
   blender and then measure each tablespoon of honey, and add it to
   the mixture. Point to the appropriate button, or refer to it by color,
   and have the child turn the appliance on. As the mixture blends,
   have the child taste some honey and describe the taste. Ask him or
   her to name items that taste similar to honey.

4. Refer to the mugs. Take the forefinger of the child's dominant
   hand (the one used for eating) and guide it to trace around the top
   edge of the mug. Say, "This is the shape of the letter *O*. It is the
   first letter in the word *oatmeal*, as in *oatmeal drink*."

5. If the child can manage it, have him or her pour the drink into the mugs.

6. As you sip the drink, discuss the activities, having the child recall the steps of preparation in sequence. If necessary, assist by asking such questions as "What did we do next?" "Then what did we do?"

# Skills

## MOTOR

- opening oatmeal packets
- measuring and pouring ingredients
- using forefinger to trace the rim of the mug

## LANGUAGE

- naming equipment and ingredients
- using number words
- describing the shape of the letter O
- describing the taste of honey
- relating sequence of activities to prepare recipe

## COGNITIVE

- recognizing the taste of honey and foods having a similar taste
- counting
- measuring ingredients
- reviewing the sequence of activities

# P is for Popcorn

## EQUIPMENT

Popcorn popper or pot with cover
1/3-cup measure
Tablespoon measure
Serving bowls

## RECIPE

1/3 cup popcorn
2 tablespoons cooking oil
   Butter-flavored salt, or salt and butter (or margarine)

Place oil in popper or pot. When heated, add popcorn.
If using pot, keep covered and shake until all corn is popped.

# Activities

1. Review with the child the names of all the equipment and
   ingredients, pointing to each: popper (pot), one-third
   cup measure, tablespoon measure, bowls, popcorn, cooking oil,
   butter-flavored salt (salt, butter, or margarine).

2. Have the child rub a little cooking oil from the cap of the container
   between a thumb and forefinger and describe the "oily" feeling.

3. Have him or her measure the oil, count each tablespoonful, and
   place it in the popper or pot. Then have the child measure and add
   the popcorn.

4. If you are using a popper, have the child turn it on and off at the
   appropriate times. If you are using a pot, you will probably finish
   shaking the popping corn yourself. Initial "pops" are usually
   spaced, so you and the child can count them together.

5. When the popping is completed, pour the corn into the bowls.
   Ask the child to touch a few kernels and describe the sensation.
   The response should be "hot" or "warm."

6. With pieces of popped corn, form the letter *P* on the counter. Say, "This is the letter *P*. It is the first letter in the word *popcorn*." Then have the child form the letter.

7. Now have the child sprinkle butter-flavored salt on the popcorn (or add melted butter and salt to the popcorn).

8. As you enjoy what some Spanish-speaking people call *palomitas* (little doves), ask the child to describe the "salty" taste. Then discuss the activities, having the child recall the steps of preparation in sequence. If necessary, assist by asking such questions as "What did we do next?" "Then what did we do?"

# Skills

## MOTOR

- removing and replacing cooking oil cap
- measuring and pouring ingredients
- turning popper on and off
- arranging popped corn to form the letter P

## LANGUAGE

- naming equipment and ingredients
- using number words
- describing textures and temperatures; oily, warm, hot
- describing the "salty" taste
- naming the letter P
- relating sequence of activities to prepare recipe

## COGNITIVE

- counting
- identifying textures and temperatures; oily, warm, hot
- recognizing the "salty" taste
- measuring ingredients
- reviewing the sequence of activities

# Q is for Quick Muffins

## EQUIPMENT

Cup measure                    Paper towel or napkin
Large spoon                    Muffin tin
Mixing bowl

## RECIPE

2 cups self-rising flour
1 pint softened vanilla ice cream
  Shortening or cooking oil
  Squeeze margarine

Combine the flour and ice cream in the mixing bowl, stirring until smooth. Fill greased muffin cups three-fourths full. Bake in hot 425° oven for twenty minutes, or until muffins are golden brown. Makes twelve large muffins.

# Activities

1. Review with the child the names of all the equipment and ingredients, pointing to each: cup measure, spoon, muffin tin, mixing bowl, paper towel or napkin, flour, ice cream, shortening (cooking oil), squeeze margarine.

2. Have the child measure two cups of flour and, counting each, pour them into the mixing bowl.

3. Have him or her open the carton of ice cream and spoon the contents into the bowl.

4. Then have the child stir the mixture until it is smooth, assisting if necessary.

5. Next have him or her grease the muffin tin with shortening or cooking oil, using a paper towel or napkin. Explain that this is done so that the muffins will not stick to the tin.

6. Have the child count the number of muffin holes in the tin. If he or she cannot yet count to twelve, count with the child as far as he or she can go, then complete the count yourself.

7. Have the child spoon the mixture into the holes, indicating the three-fourths level to fill. Explain that this will allow space for the muffins to expand as they bake. (When they are done, point out how the muffins have "grown.")

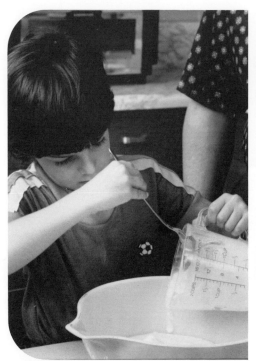

8. When the muffins are baked, empty them onto a plate. Now, using the squeeze margarine, form the letter *Q* on the bottom of a muffin. Say, "This is the letter *Q*. It is the first letter of the word *quick*, as in *quick muffins*." If the child can manage it, have him or her form a *Q* with the margarine on the bottom of another muffin.

9. As you eat the muffins, maybe with milk, discuss the activities, having the child recall the steps of preparation in sequence. If necessary, assist by asking such questions as "What did we do next?" "Then what did we do?"

78

# Skills

## MOTOR

- stirring
- opening and closing containers
- measuring and pouring ingredients
- greasing muffin tin
- transferring batter from bowl to muffin tin
- forming the letter Q

## LANGUAGE

- naming equipment and ingredients
- using number words
- naming the letter Q
- relating sequence of activities to prepare recipe

## COGNITIVE

- counting
- measuring ingredients
- recognizing fractional parts; three-fourths
- reviewing the sequence of activities

# R is for
# Raisin Rocks

## EQUIPMENT

Large mixing bowl            Small bowl
Wooden spoon                 Teaspoon
Paper towel or napkin        Cookie sheet
Sifter                       Cup measure

## RECIPE

1 package spice cake mix (2-layer size)
1 cup raisins
1 4½-ounce container whipped topping, thawed
2 eggs
1 cup powdered sugar, sifted
  Shortening or cooking oil

Combine cake mix, raisins, topping, and eggs. Drop by
teaspoonfuls in powdered sugar. Place on greased cookie
sheet (cookies spread out as they bake) and bake at 350° for
fifteen minutes.

# Activities

1. Review with the child the names of all the equipment and
   ingredients, pointing to each: mixing bowl, wooden spoon, sifter,
   cup measure, paper towel or napkin, small bowl, teaspoon, cookie
   sheet, cake mix, raisins, topping, eggs, shortening (cooking oil),
   powdered sugar.

2. Have the child open the cake mix box and pour the contents into
   the large mixing bowl.

3. Next, have the child open the raisin box and pour some raisins
   onto the counter. Separate them and arrange the raisins to form
   the letter *R*. Say, "This is the letter *R*. It is the first letter in the
   words *raisin* and *rocks*, as in *raisin rocks*." Now have the child
   form the letter.

4. Have the child measure and pour a cup of raisins into the mixing bowl. Then have him or her open the container of topping and add the contents to the mixture.

5. Together, count the eggs. Demonstrate how to crack an egg and add it to the bowl. Have the child crack and add the second egg.

6. Now have the child stir the mixture with the wooden spoon until all the ingredients are thoroughly combined.

7. Using shortening or cooking oil and a paper towel, have the child grease the cookie sheet. Explain that this is done to prevent the raisin rocks from sticking to the sheet.

8. Have him or her measure a cup of powdered sugar into the sifter. Demonstrate the use of the sifter, if necessary, and have the child sift the sugar into the small bowl. Then show how to drop the cookie batter by teaspoonfuls into the powdered sugar and coat thoroughly. Let the child complete the task.

9. Help the child place the coated balls on the cookie sheet and count them as you work. Count with the child as far as he or she can go, completing the count yourself if necessary. Now bake at 350° for fifteen minutes.

10. While munching the raisin rocks, discuss the activities, having the child recall the steps of preparation in sequence. If necessary, assist by asking such questions as "What did we do next?" "Then what did we do?"

# Skills

## MOTOR
- stirring
- sifting
- greasing cookie sheet
- measuring and pouring ingredients
- cracking eggs and emptying contents
- opening packages
- arranging raisins to form the letter R
- dropping batter by teaspoonfuls

## LANGUAGE
- naming equipment and ingredients
- using number words
- naming the letter R
- relating sequence of activities to prepare recipe

## COGNITIVE
- counting
- measuring ingredients
- reviewing the sequence of activities

# S is for Sandwich

## EQUIPMENT

Knife
Pastry brush
Plates

## RECIPE

4 slices bread
  Salad dressing or mayonnaise
2 slices luncheon meat (round)
2 slices cheese (square)
2 slices tomato
2 leaves lettuce
  Additional or substitute ingredients you or the child
  may wish.

# Activities

1. Place the items in a row in the order listed above.

2. Review with the child the names of all the equipment and
   ingredients, pointing to each: pastry brush, knife, plates, bread,
   salad dressing (mayonnaise), luncheon meat (or by name),
   cheese, tomato, lettuce (other ingredients).

3. Discuss the tastes and colors of the bread, salad dressing
   (mayonnaise), meat, cheese, tomatoes, lettuce, and any other
   ingredients. Ask the child to name items with similar tastes, and
   find objects of similar colors in the room.

4. Count the items with the child, completing the count yourself
   if necessary.

5. Say, "When we make a sandwich, the first thing we usually do is
   spread the dressing (mayonnaise) on the bread. But this time we
   shall do it in a special way." Dip the pastry brush in the salad
   dressing (mayonnaise) and brush the letter S on a slice of bread.

Then say, "This is the letter *S*. It is the first letter in the word *sandwich*." Now have the child brush the letter on another slice of bread. Guide the hand as necessary.

6. Say, "Now that the dressing (mayonnaise) is on the bread, what comes next?" As the child places the meat on the bread ask, "Is the meat the same shape as the bread?" Talk about the meanings of "square" and "round." Point out corners and curved edges.

7. With each step, say "What is next?" As the child lifts the cheese say, "Is the cheese shaped like the bread or the meat?" (If necessary, have the child place the cheese on the meat and on the bread to compare shapes.) "What do we call the shape of the cheese?"

8. Continue until the sandwich is prepared, in each case discussing the shape of the item added, finishing with the second slice of bread.

9. Have the child make a second sandwich. Discuss shapes again if you wish.

10. As you enjoy the sandwiches, perhaps with milk, discuss the activities, having the child recall the steps of preparation in sequence. If necessary, assist by asking such questions as "What did we do next?" "Then what did we do?"

# Skills

## MOTOR

- forming the letter S
- placing ingredients on the sandwich

## LANGUAGE

- naming equipment and ingredients
- naming colors
- describing tastes
- using number words
- describing shapes
- naming the letter S
- relating sequence of activities to prepare recipe

## COGNITIVE

- identifying colors and objects of similar colors
- recognizing tastes and foods having similar tastes
- recognizing and comparing shapes; square, round
- counting
- reviewing the sequence of activities

# **T** *is for* **Toast**

**EQUIPMENT**

Broiler
Knife

**RECIPE**

2 slices bread
　Squeeze margarine
　Sugar
　Cinnamon

Spread margarine, then sprinkle sugar and cinnamon on slices of bread. Toast under broiler.

# Activities

1. Review with the child the names of all the equipment and ingredients, pointing to each: broiler, knife, bread, margarine, sugar, cinnamon.

2. Call attention to the colors and tastes of the margarine, sugar, and cinnamon. Have the child think of other items with similar colors and tastes.

3. Using the squeeze margarine, form the letter *T* on one slice of bread. Say, "This is the letter *T*. It is the first letter in the word *toast.*"

4. Have the child use the margarine to repeat the process on the other slice of bread. Then have him or her use the knife to spread out the margarine, still keeping the form of the *T*.

5. Now have the child sprinkle sugar and cinnamon on the *T* shape.

6. Place both slices of bread under the broiler until the *T* is melted and bubbly.

7. As you eat the toast, discuss the activities, having the child recall the steps of preparation in sequence. If necessary, assist by asking such questions as "What did we do next?" "Then what did we do?"

# Skills

## MOTOR
- using the margarine to form the letter T
- spreading margarine
- sprinkling sugar and cinnamon

## LANGUAGE
- naming equipment and ingredients
- naming colors
- describing tastes
- naming the letter T
- relating sequence of activities to prepare recipe

## COGNITIVE
- identifying colors and objects of similar colors
- recognizing tastes and foods having similar tastes
- reviewing the sequence of activities

# U *is for* Upside Down Cake

## EQUIPMENT

Medium-sized mixing bowl    ⅔-cup measure
9″ x 9″ baking dish or pan    Tablespoon measure
Knife    ¼-teaspoon measure
Spoon or whisk

## RECIPE

1 8½-ounce can pineapple chunks
1 bottle maraschino cherries
⅔ cup brown sugar
1 tablespoon flour
¼ teaspoon cinnamon
¼ teaspoon salt
1 stick margarine
1 package yellow cake mix (1-layer size)

Place pineapple chunks and cherries in a greased 9″ x 9″ baking dish or pan. Blend dry ingredients together in mixing bowl and pour over fruit. Chip margarine over mixture. Follow cake mix directions on package and pour batter over mixture in pan. Bake at 350° for twenty-five minutes or until done.

# Activities

1. Review with the child the names of all the equipment and ingredients, pointing to each: mixing bowl, baking dish or pan, knife, spoon, two-thirds cup measure, tablespoon measure, one-fourth teaspoon measure, pineapple chunks, maraschino cherries, brown sugar, flour, cinnamon, salt, margarine, cake mix.

2. If he or she is able, have the child open the can of pineapple, the bottle of maraschino cherries, the cake mix, and unwrap the margarine.

3. Have the child taste the flour, brown sugar, salt, cinnamon, and margarine. Then have him or her try to name items with similar tastes.

4. Discuss the colors of the flour, brown sugar, cinnamon, salt, margarine, cake mix, pineapple, and cherries. Ask the child to find items of similar colors in the kitchen.

5. Have the child measure and add the brown sugar, flour, cinnamon, and salt to the mixing bowl, and combine the ingredients by stirring.

6. Use a square of margarine to grease the pan and form the letter *U* on the bottom. Say "This is the letter *U*. It is the first letter in the word *upside*, as in *upside down cake*."

7. Instruct the child to place the pineapple chunks over the buttered *U* shape. Then ask him or her to place the cherries next to the pineapple chunks, on the inside of the letter. Then have the child arrange another row of pineapple chunks inside the cherries. Together, count the cherries and the pineapple chunks. Count with the child as far as he or she can go completing the count yourself if necessary.

8. Have the child pour the dry mixture over the fruit. Then help him or her chip margarine over the top.

9. Guide the child in the preparation of the cake mix, and have him or her pour it into the pan. Bake at 350° for twenty-five minutes or until done.

10. As you wait for the cake to bake, or as you eat it, discuss the activities, having the child recall the steps of preparation in sequence. If necessary, assist by asking such questions as "What did we do next?" "Then what did we do?"

# Skills

## MOTOR

- stirring
- opening containers
- measuring and pouring ingredients
- arranging pineapple chunks and cherries to form the letter U

## LANGUAGE

- naming equipment and ingredients
- describing tastes
- naming colors
- using number words
- naming the letter U
- relating sequence of activities to prepare recipe

## COGNITIVE

- counting
- measuring ingredients
- identifying colors and objects of similar colors
- recognizing tastes and foods having similar tastes
- reviewing the sequence of activities

# $\mathbb{V}$ *is for* **Vegetable Soup**

## EQUIPMENT

Saucepan
Paring knife
Vegetable peeler
V-shaped cookie cutter

(If not available locally, letter-shaped cookie cutters can be obtained from Wilton Enterprises, Inc., 833 West 115th Street, Chicago, Illinois, 60643.)

## RECIPE

2 potatoes
1 onion
1 carrot
1 stalk celery
1 8-ounce can tomato sauce
  Alphabet macaroni
  Seasonings as desired

Peel potatoes and onion, scrape carrot. Cut carrot and celery into bite-sized pieces and chop onion. Place in one quart of water in saucepan. Add tomato sauce and seasonings as desired and pieces of potato sliced and cut in V-shapes. Cook on medium heat until vegetables are tender. Add marcaroni.

# Activities

1. Review with the child the names of all the equipment and ingredients, pointing to each: saucepan, cookie cutter, paring knife, vegetable peeler, potatoes, carrot, onion, celery, tomato sauce, macaroni, seasonings (as desired).

2. Peel the potatoes and the onion and scrape the carrot, or have the child do so if he or she can manage it. Have the child cut the carrots and the celery into bite-sized pieces and, if able, chop

the onion. Then have him or her add all the ingredients, except the potatoes, to the pan.

3. Cut, or have the child cut the potatoes into length-wise slices about one-quarter inch thick. Then, using the cookie cutter, cut the letter *V* from one of the slices. Say, "This is the letter *V*. It is the first letter in the word *vegetable,* as in *vegetable soup.*" Now have the child cut the remaining *V*s from the potato slices.

4. When cutting is completed, have the child add the potatoes to the pan.

5. Have the child open the can of tomato sauce, if he or she can manage it, and add the contents to the pan.

6. Call attention to the colors of the potatoes (inside and out), onion, carrot, celery, and tomato sauce. Ask him or her to find objects of similar colors in the room.

7. Add seasonings as you and the child desire.

8. As the vegetables become tender and the soup nears completion, have the child add some alphabet macaroni. Have him or her find the letter *V* and other familiar letters.

9. As you taste the soup, discuss the activities, having the child recall the steps of preparation in sequence. If necessary, assist by asking such questions as "What did we do next?" "Then what did we do?"

# Skills

### MOTOR
- peeling, cutting, scraping, chopping
- using cookie cutter to form the letter V
- opening can
- sorting alphabet macaroni

### LANGUAGE
- naming equipment and ingredients
- naming colors
- naming the letter V
- relating sequence of activities to prepare recipe

### COGNITIVE
- identifying colors and objects of similar colors
- identifying the letter V and other familiar letters
- reviewing the sequence of activities

# W is for Watermelon

## EQUIPMENT

Knife
Plates
Spoons or forks

## RECIPE

Cut watermelon in half, widthwise. Cut from either side slices of desired thickness. Place on plates.

# Activities

1. Review with the child the names of all the equipment and ingredients, pointing to each: knife, plates, spoons (forks), watermelon.

2. Have the child run his or her hand over the outside of the watermelon and describe how the surface feels. Ask him or her to name other things that feel smooth.

3. Cut the watermelon in half, widthwise. Now discuss the inside and outside colors and the color of the seeds. Ask the child to find objects of similar colors in the room.

4. Place a slice of watermelon on a plate and cut a piece from each side—a small triangle from the bottom, and two small triangles from the top to form the letter *W*. Say, "This is the letter *W*. It is the first letter in the word *watermelon.*" Now have the child cut out a *W*.

5. For additional instruction, you might have the child use seeds to form *W*s on another plate.

6. As you enjoy the watermelon, discuss the activities, having the child recall the steps of preparation in sequence. If necessary, assist by asking such questions as "What did we do next?" "Then what did we do?"

# Skills

## MOTOR

- forming the letter W
- arranging seeds

## LANGUAGE

- naming equipment and ingredients
- naming colors
- describing the texture of the watermelon
- naming the letter W
- relating sequence of activities to prepare recipe

## COGNITIVE

- indentifying colors and objects of similar colors
- recognizing a smooth texture and objects having a similar texture
- reviewing the sequence of activities

# X is for X-tra Recipes

# Chocolate Pudding

## EQUIPMENT

Quart jar
Cup measure
Spoon
Pudding cups (bowls)

## RECIPE

1 package instant chocolate pudding mix
2 cups cold milk

Pour pudding mix and milk into quart jar. Cover tightly and shake until thoroughly mixed. Spoon into pudding cups. Allow to set until firm.

# Activities

1. Review with the child the names of all the equipment and ingredients, pointing to each: pudding mix, milk, quart jar, cup measure, spoon, pudding cups (bowls).

2. Have the child open the box of pudding mix and pour the contents into the jar. Then have him or her measure the milk, counting each cup, and add to the pudding mix. Discuss the colors of the milk and mix, and ask the child to point out objects of similar colors in the kitchen.

3. Now have the child place the cover on the jar—check to see that it is tight—and shake the mixture until it is ready. Count the shakes with the child, counting with him or her as far as he or she can go. Then complete the count yourself if necessary.

4. Have the child open the jar and spoon the pudding into the cups.

5. As the pudding sets, discuss the activities, having the child recall the steps of preparation in sequence. If necessary, assist by asking such questions as "What did we do next?" "Then what did we do?"

# Skills

## MOTOR

- pouring
- shaking
- opening and closing jar
- measuring
- spooning out pudding

## LANGUAGE

- naming equipment and ingredients
- using number words
- naming colors
- relating sequence of activities to prepare recipe

## COGNITIVE

- measuring ingredients
- counting
- identifying colors and objects of similar colors
- reviewing the sequence of activities

# Shortcake

## EQUIPMENT

Tablespoon measure          Mixing bowl
Cookie sheet                Large spoon
Paper towel or napkin       Beater or electric mixer

## RECIPE

1 10-ounce can refrigerated biscuits
2 tablespoons butter, melted
2 to 4 tablespoons sugar
½ pint whipping cream
1 pint fresh or frozen strawberries, sliced and sweetened
    Shortening or cooking oil

Separate biscuit dough into ten biscuits. Gently press two biscuits together for each shortcake. Dip top and sides of each in melted butter, then in sugar. Place on greased cookie sheet and bake fourteen to seventeen minutes, or until golden brown. Cool slightly. Whip cream, split biscuits and fill with strawberries and cream. Top with additional berries and whipped cream.

# Activities

1. Review with the child the names of all the equipment and ingredients: tablespoon measure, cookie sheet, beater or electric mixer, shortening (cooking oil), mixing bowl, spoon, strawberries, biscuits, butter, sugar, whipping cream, paper towel or napkin.

2. If he or she can manage it, have the child open the packages of frozen strawberries and the can of biscuits. If using fresh strawberries, share the task of removing the stems and slicing the berries.

3. Have the child measure the butter and place it in a pan for melting, and have him or her measure the sugar into a shallow dish.

4. Have the child use shortening or cooking oil and a paper towel or napkin to grease the cookie sheet. Explain that this prevents the shortcake from sticking to the sheet.

5. Working together, separate the biscuits and press two together for each shortcake. Dip the biscuits into the butter, then the sugar, and place them on the greased sheet.

6. Discuss the colors of the strawberries, butter, sugar, and biscuit dough. Ask the child to locate objects of similar colors in the room. Discuss the tastes of strawberries, butter, and sugar and ask the child to suggest items with similar tastes.

7. Count the biscuits with the child, completing the count yourself if necessary.

8. As the biscuits bake, have the child open the carton of whipping cream and pour the contents into the mixing bowl. If you use a hand beater, demonstrate its use to the child, and let him or her try whipping the cream. Be prepared to finish the whipping yourself. If you use an electric mixer, show the child which buttons to push. As the beating progresses, add the sugar to taste.

9. When the biscuits are ready, let the child help in separating them, filling with strawberries and whipped cream, and topping with additional berries and cream.

10. As you treat yourself to the shortcake, discuss the activities, having the child recall the steps of preparation in sequence. If necessary, assist by asking such questions as "What did we do next?" "Then what did we do?"

# Skills

## MOTOR

- peeling paper from biscuit can
- opening packages and containers
- using hand beater
- separating and joining biscuits
- removing stems and slicing strawberries (if fresh)
- measuring and pouring
- greasing cookie sheet
- separating biscuits when done
- spooning strawberries and whipped cream onto biscuits

## LANGUAGE

- naming equipment and ingredients
- naming colors
- using number words
- describing tastes
- relating sequence of activities to prepare recipe

## COGNITIVE

- measuring ingredients
- counting
- identifying colors and objects of similar colors
- recognizing tastes and foods having similar tastes
- reviewing the sequence of activities

# Thumbprint Cookies

## EQUIPMENT

Cup measure
½-cup measure
¼-cup measure
½-teaspoon measure
¼-teaspoon measure
Sifter

Mixing bowl
Wooden spoon
Beater or electric mixer
Paper towel or napkin
Cookie sheet
Egg separator (optional)

## RECIPE

¼ cup shortening
¼ cup butter
¼ cup brown sugar
1 egg, separated
½ teaspoon vanilla
1 cup flour, sifted
¼ teaspoon salt
　　Chopped nuts
　　Jelly or powdered sugar icing (if desired)

Combine shortening, butter, sugar, egg yolk, and vanilla; mix thoroughly. Sift flour and salt into mixture and stir. Roll mixture into one-inch balls and roll in lightly beaten egg white, then in nuts. Place on greased cookie sheet and bake at 375° for five minutes. Remove from oven and quickly press thumb gently into top of each cookie. Bake for eight minutes longer. Jelly or powdered sugar icing may be placed in each thumb print if desired.

# Activities

1. Review with the child the names of all the equipment and ingredients, pointing to each: cup measure, one-half cup measure, one-fourth cup measure, one-half teaspoon measure, one-fourth

teaspoon measure, sifter, mixing bowl, wooden spoon, egg separator (optional), beater or electric mixer, paper towel or napkin, cookie sheet, shortening, butter, brown sugar, egg, vanilla, flour, salt, chopped nuts, jelly or powdered sugar icing (if desired).

2. Discuss the colors of the ingredients, and have the child point out objects of similar colors in the room. Then ask the child to name items with similar tastes.

3. Have the child measure the shortening, butter, and brown sugar, and add them to the mixing bowl. Then demonstrate the egg separator, or the means of separating egg parts by carefully pouring from one half of the shell into the other. Have the child do this if he or she is able. Discuss the white and yolk and their colors.

4. Add the yolk to the mixture and have the child measure and add the vanilla. Talk about the smell of vanilla.

5. Demonstrate the sifter, and have the child measure the flour and sugar into it and sift the contents into the bowl. Stir the mixture.

6. Have the child use some shortening and a paper towel or napkin to grease the cookie sheet. Explain that this is done so the cookies will not stick to the sheet.

7. Both you and the child roll the mixture into balls and place them on the greased sheet. Count them with the child as far as he or she can go, completing the count yourself if necessary.

8. As the cookies bake, demonstrate the hand beater to the child and have him or her lightly beat the egg white. If you use an electric mixer, show the child which buttons to push.

9. Both you and the child can make thumb impressions in the cookies. Fill the impressions with jelly or powdered sugar icing, if desired.

10. As you eat the cookies, discuss the activities, having the child recall the steps of preparation in sequence. If necessary, assist by asking such questions as "What did we do next?" "Then what did we do?"

# Skills

## MOTOR

- stirring
- greasing cookie sheet
- sifting
- using hand beater
- measuring and pouring ingredients
- cracking and separating eggs
- rolling mixture into balls
- placing balls on cookie sheet
- pressing thumb into cookies

## LANGUAGE

- naming equipment and ingredients
- using number words
- naming colors
- describing tastes
- describing the smell of vanilla
- relating sequence of activities to prepare recipe

## COGNITIVE

- counting
- measuring ingredients
- identifying colors and objects of similar colors
- recognizing tastes and foods having similar tastes
- recognizing the smell of vanilla and items having a similar smell
- reviewing the sequence of activities

# Wheatgerm Bread

## EQUIPMENT

Cup measure
½-cup measure
¼-cup measure
Teaspoon measure
Tablespoon measure

Mixing bowl
Small saucepan
Baking pan
Large spoon
Paper towel or napkin

## RECIPE

1 cup warm milk
½ cup honey
¼ cup cooking oil or butter
2 eggs
1 teaspoon salt
1 tablespoon baking powder
½ cup wheatgerm
3 or more cups unbleached flour
Shortening

Combined warm milk, honey, oil, eggs, salt, baking powder, and wheatgerm in mixing bowl. Knead in enough flour to make the dough non-sticky. Divide into eight balls. Pat into oval shapes about the size of a hand and make finger and thumb impressions in the dough as desired. Grease pan and bake at 350° for fifteen to twenty minutes.

# Activities

1. Review with the child the names of all the equipment and ingredients, pointing to each: cup measure, one-half cup measure, one-fourth cup measure, teaspoon measure, tablespoon measure, mixing bowl, saucepan, baking pan, spoon, paper towel or napkin, milk, honey, cooking oil (butter), eggs, salt, baking powder, wheatgerm, flour, shortening.

2. Have the child note the colors and tastes of the ingredients. Ask him or her to name items of similar tastes, and point out things of similar colors in the kitchen.

3. Have the child measure the milk into the saucepan for heating. Then have him or her measure the honey and oil (or butter) and add those ingredients, with the milk, to the mixing bowl. Demonstrate how to crack an egg and add the contents, having the child duplicate the process with the other egg. Count the eggs with the child. Now have him or her measure and add the salt, baking powder, and wheatgerm to the bowl.

4. Demonstrate kneading, and practice the motions with the child.

5. Using shortening and a paper towel or napkin, have the child grease the baking pan.

6. Together, divide the mixture into eight balls. Count them with the child as far as he or she can go, completing the count yourself if necessary.

7. Now both of you pat the balls into oval shapes. Note the shape, and ask the child to point out objects with a similar shape in the room. Then make whatever impressions the two of you wish in the dough with fingers and thumbs, and bake at 350° for fifteen to twenty minutes.

8. As you and the child enjoy the bread with butter, and perhaps jelly, discuss the activities, having the child recall the steps of preparation in sequence. If necessary, assist by asking such questions as "What did we do next?" "Then what did we do?"

# Skills

## MOTOR

- stirring
- greasing baking pan
- measuring and pouring ingredients
- kneading dough
- rolling dough into balls
- patting balls into oval shapes
- making finger and thumb impressions in dough
- placing dough in pan

## LANGUAGE

- naming equipment and ingredients
- using number words
- naming colors
- describing tastes
- relating sequence of activities to prepare recipe

## COGNITIVE

- measuring ingredients
- counting
- identifying colors and objects of similar colors
- recognizing tastes and foods having similar tastes
- identifying an oval shape and objects having a similar shape
- reviewing the sequence of activities

# Y *is for*
# Yeast Biscuits

## EQUIPMENT

2 mixing bowls                    Baking sheet
⅓-cup measure                     Spoon
2½-inch round biscuit cutter      Rolling pin
Pastry board

## RECIPE

1 5½-ounce package biscuit mix
1 package dry yeast
⅓ cup warm water
  Flour

Pour biscuit mix into mixing bowl. Dissolve yeast in one-third cup warm water and add to mix. Knead thoroughly on floured board, roll out and cut into biscuits. Place on ungreased baking sheet and bake at 450° for eight to ten minutes.

# Activities

1. Review with the child the names of all the equipment and ingredients, pointing to each: mixing bowls, one-third cup measure, biscuit cutter, pastry board, baking sheet, rolling pin, spoon, biscuit mix, dry yeast, water, flour.

2. Have the child open the package of biscuit mix and pour the contents into the bowl. Then have him or her draw one-third cup of warm water from the tap, open the yeast package, pour contents into second mixing bowl, and stir until it is dissolved. Have the child add the ingredients to the biscuit mix and stir.

3. When ingredients are thoroughly mixed, have the child sprinkle flour on the pastry board. Then place the dough on the board and demonstrate how to knead it, pulling the dough from the top with the fingers and pushing it away with the heels of the hands, mixing in more flour in the process. Now have the child take over the kneading.

4. When finished kneading, show how to sprinkle flour on the dough and roll it out with the rolling pin. Then have the child roll out the dough to about one-half inch thickness.

5. After dipping the cutter in flour, cut out a biscuit. Have the child cut out the remainder of the dough and place each biscuit on the sheet. Have him or her count the biscuits as far as he or she can go. Complete the count yourself if necessary.

6. Place the biscuits in the oven to bake at 450° for eight to ten minutes.

7. While the biscuits are baking, have the child gather the leftover dough and roll and pat it into a string. Then have him or her divide it into three pieces, one somewhat longer than the other two. Guide the child to form the three pieces into the letter *Y*. Say, "This is the letter *Y*. It is the first letter in the word *yeast*, as in *yeast biscuits*."

8. As you eat the biscuits with butter or margarine, and perhaps jelly or jam, discuss the activities, having the child recall the steps of preparation in sequence. If necessary, assist by asking such questions as "What did we do next?" "Then what did we do?"

# Skills

## MOTOR
- using rolling pin
- opening and emptying packages
- measuring and pouring water
- sprinkling flour
- stirring
- kneading
- using cutter
- placing biscuits on sheet
- shaping dough
- forming the letter Y

## LANGUAGE
- naming equipment and ingredients
- using number words
- naming the letter Y
- relating sequence of activities to prepare recipe

## COGNITIVE
- measuring ingredients
- counting
- reviewing the sequence of activities

# Z is for
# Zoo Cookies

## EQUIPMENT

Mixing bowl
¼-cup measure
Wooden spoon
Cookie sheet

Animal-shaped cookie cutters
Pastry board
Rolling pin

## RECIPE

1 package cake mix (2-layer size)
¼ cup margarine or butter
2 eggs
  Flour

Pour half of the cake mix into mixing bowl. Add butter and eggs and combine thoroughly. Stir in remainder of cake mix. Chill if necessary. Roll out on floured pastry board to about one-eighth inch thickness. Cut out shapes, place on ungreased cookie sheet, and bake at 375° for eight to ten minutes.

# Activities

1. Review with the child the names of all the equipment and ingredients, pointing to each: mixing bowl, wooden spoon, cookie sheet, cookie cutters, pastry board, rolling pin, one-fourth cup measure, cake mix, margarine (butter), eggs, flour.

2. Have the child open the package of cake mix and pour half the contents into the mixing bowl. Then have him or her measure and add the margarine or butter.

3. Next, count the eggs, and demonstrate how to crack one and add the contents to the bowl. Discuss the colors of yolks and whites. Have the child crack and add the second egg. Then have him or her stir the ingredients with the wooden spoon, combining thoroughly. Now have the child stir in the remainder of the cake mix.

4. Have the child sprinkle flour lightly on the pastry board and then place the dough on the board. Demonstrate the rolling pin and then have the child roll out the dough to about one-eighth inch thickness.

5. Show the child the cookie cutters and ask how many animals he or she can identify from the shapes. Cut out one or two shapes, and then let the child begin cutting out animal shapes from the dough.

6. Place one unbaked cookie at each corner of the cookie sheet. Point to the one at the upper left-hand corner and direct the child to place cookies in a line from there to the upper right-hand corner, then in a diagonal line to the lower left-hand corner, and finally on a line to the lower right-hand corner, forming the letter Z. Say, "This is the letter Z. It is the first letter in the word *zoo*, and *zoo cookies*."

7. Now place the cookies in the oven and bake at 375° for eight to ten minutes.

8. While the cookies bake, or as you snack on them, discuss the activities, having the child recall the steps of preparation in sequence. If necessary, assist by asking such questions as "What did we do next?" "Then what did we do?"

# Skills

## MOTOR
- using rolling pin
- stirring
- opening and pouring cake mix
- measuring margarine or butter
- cracking egg
- sprinkling flour
- using cookie cutter
- placing and arranging cookies on cookie sheet

## LANGUAGE
- naming equipment and ingredients
- using number words
- naming colors
- naming the letter Z
- relating sequence of activities to prepare recipe

## COGNITIVE
- measuring ingredients
- counting
- identifying colors and objects of similar color
- identifying animal shapes
- reviewing the sequence of activities

# Favorite Recipes